Barbara
To

Pat
From

Afternoon Tea, Oct. 9, 2013
Date

Sharing a Cup of Friendship

PAINTINGS BY

Sandy Lynam Clough

HARVEST HOUSE PUBLISHERS
EUGENE, OREGON

Sharing a Cup of Friendship

Text copyright © 2013 by Harvest House Publishers. Original text by Peggy Wright.
Artwork copyright © 2013 by Sandy Clough

Published by Harvest House Publishers
Eugene, Oregon 97402
www.harvesthousepublishers.com

ISBN 978-0-7369-5177-7

Design and production by Garborg Design Works, Savage, Minnesota

Harvest House Publishers has made every effort to trace the ownership of all poems and quotes. In the event of a question arising from the use of a poem or quote, we regret any error made and will be pleased to make the necessary correction in future editions of this book.

Printed in China

13 14 15 16 17 18 19 20 / LP / 10 9 8 7 6 5 4 3 2 1

A Cup of Friendship for My...

Where there's tea there's hope.
SIR ARTHUR PINERO

My Sweet Friend

KIND AND GOOD

Come and sit with me in the afternoon sunshine. Sip your tea and share what's on your generous heart. You must know I savor your thoughts as much as I am blessed by your gentle kindness. You refresh my soul and restore my joy. You are my sweet friend—so kind and good!

Cranberry Lemon Scones
❧ SERVE WITH EARL GREY TEA ❧

CRANBERRY LEMON SCONES

2 cups all-purpose flour
6 tablespoons sugar, divided
1 tablespoon baking powder
1 teaspoon salt
2 teaspoons lemon zest
6 tablespoons cold butter, diced

2 eggs, lightly beaten
½ cup heavy cream
¾ cup fresh cranberries, chopped
1 egg beaten with 1 tablespoon water for egg wash
½ cup powdered sugar
4 teaspoons lemon juice

Preheat oven to 400 degrees. In a large mixing bowl, whisk together flour, 5 tablespoons sugar, baking powder, salt, and lemon zest. Add the butter and mix, using your hands, until the butter is the size of peas. Mix the eggs and heavy cream together and then pour into the flour and butter mixture. Mix until just combined. Do not overmix. Stir in the cranberries.

Place the dough on a well-floured surface and knead it into a ball. Roll the dough until it is about 3/4-inch thick. Flour a 3-inch round cookie cutter and cut circles of dough. Reroll out extra dough and cut more circles. Place the scones on a baking sheet lined with parchment paper. Brush scones with the egg wash, then sprinkle with remaining 1 tablespoon sugar and bake for 20 minutes, or until the tops are lightly browned. Do not overbake. Allow the scones to cool for 20 minutes.

While the scones are cooling, whisk together the powdered sugar and lemon juice and drizzle over scones once cool. Makes 6 scones.

He has the substance of all bliss
To whom a virtuous friend is given:
So sweet harmonious friendship is,
Add but eternity, you'll make it heaven.

JOHN NORRIS

Kindness gives birth to kindness.

SOPHOCLES

EARL GREY TEA

Traditionally Earl Grey tea is a blend of Indian and Ceylon black teas flavored with oil extracted from the rind of the bergamot orange. To make Earl Grey tea, pour 8 ounces near-boiling water over one teaspoon loose-leaf tea or one regular-sized teabag. Steep four to five minutes. Remove the leaves or teabag and enjoy. Sugar, honey, lemon, and/or milk may be added to taste.

There is a great
deal of poetry and
fine sentiment in
a chest of tea.

RALPH WALDO EMERSON

Kindness given and received aright,
and knitting two hearts into one, is a
thing of heaven, as rare in this world
as a perfect love; both are the overflow
of only very rare and beautiful souls.

HONORÉ DE BALZAC

Oh the experience of this sweet life.

DANTE

Descending from his perch, he fell to
unpacking it with great neatness and
dispatch, while Rose watched him, wondering
what was going to happen. Presently, out
from the wrappings came a teapot, which
caused her to clasp her hands with delight...
Two pretty cups with covers, and a fine
scarlet tray, completed the set, and made one
long to have a "dish of tea," even in Chinese
style, without cream or sugar.

LOUISA MAY ALCOTT, FROM *EIGHT COUSINS*

THE COZY FIRE IS BRIGHT AND GAY.

THE MERRY KETTLE BOILS AWAY

AND HUMS A CHEERFUL SONG.

I SING THE SAUCER AND THE CUP;

PRAY, MARY, FILL THE TEAPOT UP.

AND DO NOT MAKE IT STRONG.

BARRY PAIN

Friends—they are kind to each other's
hopes. They cherish each other's dreams.

HENRY DAVID THOREAU

Many kinds of fruit
grow upon the tree
of life, but none so
sweet as friendship.

LUCY LARCOM

sparrow

robin

My Faithful Friend

DEVOTED AND TRUE

You and I have shared a pot of tea
more often than I can remember. While
cradling our steaming mugs of brewed
delight and breathing in its sweet aroma,
we've celebrated life's joys, sorted out
the challenges, and nurtured a beautiful
friendship. Our time together is golden. You
are my faithful friend—so devoted and true!

Maple Oatmeal Walnut Scones
with Maple Syrup Glaze
❧ SERVE WITH GINGER PEACH TEA ❧

MAPLE OATMEAL WALNUT SCONES WITH MAPLE SYRUP GLAZE

2 cups all-purpose flour
1 cup whole wheat flour
¾ cup oats
4 teaspoons baking powder
½ teaspoon baking soda
¼ teaspoon salt
½ cup cold unsalted butter, diced
½ cup granulated sugar

1 egg
⅔ cup buttermilk
¼ cup maple syrup
½ cup chopped walnuts
coarse sugar to sprinkle on top
2 tablespoons maple syrup
1 teaspoon vanilla extract
¼ cup powdered sugar

Preheat oven to 375 degrees. Mix flours, oats, baking powder, baking soda, and salt in a large mixing bowl. Add diced butter to the flour mixture and mix until crumbly. Sprinkle sugar on top but do not mix it in. Beat egg and buttermilk in a small bowl and pour over the flour/sugar mixture. Carefully mix the milk mixture into the dry ingredients with a fork, scraping from the bottom to top in large swift sweeps. When dough is about half-mixed, add ¼ cup maple syrup and walnuts. Continue to mix until all flour is incorporated, but no further.

Form dough into a circular loaf, about 1½ inches thick, and cut into 8 triangular pieces. Sprinkle coarse sugar on top before baking. Place each triangle on a baking sheet and bake for 12 to 15 minutes. Remove from oven and allow scones to cool.

While scones are cooling, mix 2 tablespoons maple syrup, vanilla, and powdered sugar in a small bowl and drizzle over the top of cooled scones. Makes 8 scones.

Hydrangea

GINGER PEACH TEA

Ginger peach tea is quickly becoming an American favorite. Blended from either black or green tea leaves, the flavors of ginger, peach, and apricots add a sweet note to this beverage. To make one cup, steep 1 teaspoon loose-leaf ginger peach tea or 1 regular sized teabag in 8 ounces near-boiling water for 3 minutes. Remove the leaves or teabag and enjoy. If desired, add sugar, honey, and/or lemon to taste. Serve hot or iced.

Hydrangea

Of all the best things upon earth, I hold that a faithful friend is the best.

OWEN MEREDITH

THERE IS NO FRIEND LIKE AN OLD FRIEND WHO HAS SHARED OUR MORNING DAYS, NO GREETING LIKE HIS WELCOME, NO HOMAGE LIKE HIS PRAISE.

OLIVER WENDELL HOLMES

magnifique

What part of confidante has that poor teapot played ever since the kindly plant was introduced among us. Why myriads of women have cried over it, to be sure!...Nature meant very kindly... when she made the tea plant; and with a little thought, what series of pictures and groups the fancy may conjure up and assemble round the teapot and cup.

WILLIAM MAKEPEACE THACKERAY

17

One sip of this will bathe
the drooping spirits in delight,
beyond the bliss of dreams.

MILTON

Friendship is a union of
spirits, a marriage of hearts,
and the bond thereof virtue.

WILLIAM PENN

There are few
hours in life
more agreeable
than the hour
dedicated to the
ceremony known
as afternoon tea.

HENRY JAMES

Hydrangea

The mind never unbends itself so agreeably as in the conversation of a well-chosen friend. There is indeed no blessing of life that is any way comparable to the enjoyment of a discreet and virtuous friend. It eases and unloads the mind, clears and improves the understanding, engenders thoughts and knowledge, animates virtue and good resolutions, soothes and allays the passions, and finds employment for most of the vacant hours of life.

JOSEPH ADDISON

magnifique

Thank God for tea!
What would the world do without tea?
How did it exist?
I am glad I was not born before tea.

REVEREND SYDNEY SMITH

My Newfound Friend

UNEXPECTED AND FRESH

The instant I heard your laughter and glimpsed the sparkle in your eyes, I knew we'd soon be the best of friends. That day was truly heaven sent. Sipping tea with you refreshes my spirit, buoys my soul, and inspires my best. You are my newfound friend—so unexpected and fresh!

Strawberries and Cream Scones
❧ SERVE WITH STRAWBERRY ICED GREEN TEA ❧

STRAWBERRIES AND CREAM SCONES

2 cups all-purpose flour
1 tablespoon baking powder
3 tablespoons sugar
½ teaspoon salt
5 tablespoons cold unsalted butter,
    cut into ¼-inch cubes

1 teaspoon grated lemon zest
1 cup diced fresh strawberries
¼ cup strawberry preserves
1 cup heavy cream
1 tablespoon lemon juice
¾ cup confectioners' sugar, sifted

Preheat oven to 425 degrees. Place flour, baking powder, sugar, and salt in the bowl of a food processor fitted with a metal blade. Process with six 1-second pulses. Remove cover of food processor and sprinkle the butter evenly over the dry ingredients. Add the grated lemon zest. Cover and process with twelve 1-second pulses. Transfer dough to a large bowl. Mix in strawberries with your hands. Add heavy cream and mix with your hands until dough begins to form. For about 10 seconds, gently knead dough by hand until it comes together into a ball. Divide dough into two equal pieces.

With lightly floured hands, press dough into two 8-inch rounds. Spread strawberry preserves over one of the rounds, leaving a half-inch outside border free of preserves. Place the other round on top of the preserve-covered round and seal edges. With a sharp knife or pizza cutter, cut the dough into 8 wedges. Place wedges on an ungreased baking sheet and bake in preheated oven 12 to 15 minutes or until tops of scones are a light brown. Transfer to a wire rack for at least 5 minutes before serving.

While the scones are cooling, make the lemon glaze by combining and mixing the lemon juice and confectioners' sugar until it's a thick, opaque icing. Drizzle over scones and serve. Makes 8 scones.

barfume

Lilac

sp

Strawberry Iced Green Tea

Especially good on a warm summer afternoon, strawberry iced green tea is refreshing and delicious. To make 6 servings, brew 6 cups green tea according to the directions on the product package. Set aside. Clean and hull 1 pint fresh strawberries and pulse in a blender until smooth. Pour strawberry puree into a medium-sized pan, add 1 cup sugar (more or less to taste), and bring to a boil. Remove from heat. Combine the strawberry puree and brewed tea in a pitcher and mix well. Chill thoroughly. Serve cold over ice.

*A true friend is
the gift of God.*

ROBERT SOUTH

Violettes

PARIS

FRANCE

splendide

To entertain a guest is to be answerable for his happiness so long as he is beneath your roof.

JEAN ANTHELME BRILLAT-SAVARIN

Blessed are they who have the gift of making friends, for it is one of God's best gifts. It involves many things, but, above all, the power of going out of one's self and seeing and appreciating whatever is noble and loving in another.

THOMAS HUGHES

Find yourself a cup of tea, the teapot is behind you. Now tell me about hundreds of things.

SAKI

THOUGH WE EAT LITTLE FLESH AND DRINK NO WINE,
YET LET'S BE MERRY; WE'LL HAVE TEA AND TOAST;
CUSTARDS FOR SUPPER, AND AN ENDLESS HOST
OF SYLLABUBS AND JELLIES AND MINCE-PIES,
AND OTHER SUCH LADYLIKE LUXURIES.

PERCY BYSSHE SHELLEY

Happiness seems made to be shared.

PIERRE CORNEILLE

Stands the church
clock at ten to three?
And is there honey
still for tea?

RUPERT BROOKE

28

VENICE

In friendship we find nothing
false or insincere; everything
is straightforward, and springs
from the heart.

Cicero

PARIS

My Rainy-Day Friend

CHEERY AND HOPEFUL

When my life reflects the feel of a gray, cloudy day, I look forward to hearing the teakettle's whistle and the delicate clinking of a spoon in a teacup. That means you are here. You always lift my spirit and brighten my outlook. You are my rainy-day friend—so cheery and hopeful!

Coconut Scones

❧ SERVE WITH TROPICAL TEA ❧

COCONUT SCONES

1 cup all-purpose flour
1 cup whole wheat pastry flour
½ cup coconut sugar
1 cup finely shredded coconut
½ teaspoon sea salt

2 teaspoons baking powder
¼ cup coconut oil, solid
⅓ cup coconut yogurt
½ cup coconut milk, full fat

Preheat oven to 375 degrees. Line a large baking sheet with a silicone mat or parchment paper and set aside. In a large bowl, whisk together the flours, sugar, coconut, salt, and baking powder. Cut in the coconut oil until the mixture resembles coarse meal. In a small bowl, stir together the yogurt and milk. Create a well in the center of the flour mixture and pour in the yogurt mixture. Scoop the dry ingredients from the bottom of the bowl and fold over the wet ingredients. Repeat this just until the mixture is combined. Do not overmix the dough. If the dough is too wet, add additional flour 1 tablespoon at a time.

Line a flat surface with parchment paper and sprinkle lightly with flour. Pat the dough into a large circle, about 1 inch thick. Using a sharp knife, cut the dough into 8 triangular segments. Transfer the dough segments to the prepared baking sheet. If desired, lightly brush each scone with melted coconut oil and sprinkle with vanilla sugar. Bake at 375 degrees for 16 to 18 minutes or until golden. Transfer to a wire rack to cool.

Scones may be stored in an air-tight container for up to 3 days. Unbaked dough can be kept frozen in the freezer. Simply place the scone segments in a freezer-safe container until ready to use. Makes 8 scones.

Tropical Tea

Similar to a fruit punch, this tea is made with several fruit juices and is best served in frosted glasses. The exotic flavors create a delicious morning wake-up or a special afternoon pick-me-up. Start by boiling 1 cup water with 1¼ cups sugar for 5 minutes to make a syrup. Next mix 3 cups freshly brewed black tea, 3 cups orange juice, 1 cup lemon juice, and 2 cups pineapple juice. Stir in the sugar syrup. Chill for several hours. When ready to serve, fill frosted glasses half full with concentrate, add ice, and top off with club soda. Makes fifteen 8-ounce servings.

MY FRIEND PEERS IN ON ME WITH MERRY
WISE FACE, AND THOUGH THE SKY STAY DIM,
THE VERY LIGHT OF DAY, THE VERY
SUN'S SELF COMES IN WITH HIM.

ALGERNON CHARLES SWINBURNE

Nowhere is the English genius
of domesticity more notably
evident than in the festival
afternoon tea. The…chink of
cups and the saucers tunes the
mind to happy repose.

GEORGE GISSING

Let us be grateful
to people who
make us happy;
they are the
charming
gardeners who
make our souls
blossom.

MARCEL PROUST

35

Tea is drunk to forget
the din of the world.
T'IEN YIHENG

Surely everyone is aware of the divine pleasures which attend a wintry fireside; candles at four o'clock, warm hearth rugs, tea, a fair tea-maker, shutters closed, curtains flowing in ample draperies to the floor, whilst the wind and rain are raging audibly without.

THOMAS DE QUINCEY

Peony

Friendship is steady
and peaceful…it
doubles our joys,
divides our griefs,
and warms our lives
with a steady flame.

CHARLES READE

Peon

Friendship is that by which the world is most blessed and receives the most good.

JEREMY TAYLOR

IF THE SIGHT OF
THE BLUE SKIES
FILLS YOU WITH JOY,
IF THE SIMPLEST
THINGS OF NATURE
HAVE A MESSAGE THAT
YOU UNDERSTAND,
REJOICE, FOR YOUR
SOUL IS ALIVE.

ELEANORA DUSE

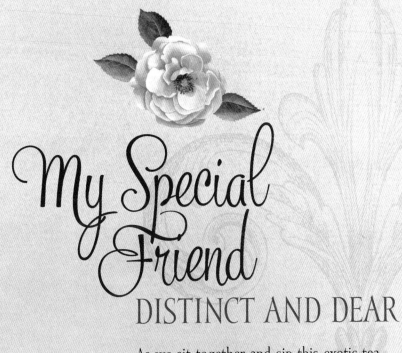

My Special Friend

DISTINCT AND DEAR

As we sit together and sip this exotic tea from treasured teacups—family heirlooms to be sure—the word *precious* comes to mind. You are precious, and I value your friendship dearly. You're like a sweet gift all wrapped up in everything extraordinary. You arc my special friend—so distinct and dear!

Chocolate Chip Orange Scones
❧ SERVE WITH ENGLISH BREAKFAST TEA ❧

CHOCOLATE CHIP ORANGE SCONES

2 cups all-purpose flour
½ cup sugar
½ teaspoon baking powder
½ teaspoon salt
½ cup butter, chilled

2 eggs
¼ cup frozen orange juice concentrate
1 teaspoon vanilla extract
1 cup mini semisweet chocolate chips

Preheat oven to 425 degrees. In a large bowl, mix together flour, sugar, baking powder, and salt. Cut the butter into small pieces on top of the flour mixture. Using a pastry blender or two knives, cut the butter into the flour mixture until it resembles coarse crumbs. In a separate bowl, stir together eggs, orange juice concentrate, and vanilla extract. Combine with the flour mixture. Dough will be very moist. With floured hands, knead in the chocolate chips until mixed well, but do not over-handle the dough.

Turn dough out onto a lightly floured cookie sheet and shape into an 8- or 9-inch circle. With a serrated knife, cut into 8 wedges. Bake for 20 to 25 minutes in a 425 degree oven.

Remove from oven and cool on a wire rack for 10 minutes. Serve warm. Makes 8 scones.

ENGLISH BREAKFAST TEA

Although the name "English breakfast tea" makes one think this black tea blend originated in England, that is not true. It is truly an American concoction. Black teas from Assam, Ceylon, and Kenya traditionally make up this popular and classic drink. To make English breakfast tea, add one teabag to 8 ounces near-boiling water and brew for 3 to 5 minutes. Sugar or honey and milk or cream are often added to this hearty tea.

The conversation
of a friend
brightens the eyes.
PERSIAN PROVERB

Ecstasy is a glass full of tea and a
piece of sugar in the mouth.
ALEXANDER PUSHKIN

Friendship, a dear balm—

Whose coming is as light and music are

'Mid dissonance and gloom—a star

Which moves not 'mid the moving heavens alone;

A smile among dark frowns: a beloved light:

A solitude, a refuge, a delight.

PERCY BYSSHE SHELLEY

45

Tea's proper use is to amuse
the idle, and relax the studious,
and dilute the full meals of
those who cannot use exercise,
and will not use abstinence.

SAMUEL JOHNSON

The path to heaven passes through a teapot.

ANCIENT PROVERB

WORDS CANNOT EXPRESS THE
JOY WHICH A FRIEND IMPARTS;
THEY ONLY CAN KNOW WHO HAVE
EXPERIENCED. A FRIEND IS DEARER
THAN THE LIGHT OF HEAVEN, FOR
IT WOULD BE BETTER FOR US THAT
THE SUN WERE EXTINGUISHED
THAN THAT WE SHOULD BE
WITHOUT FRIENDS.

SAINT JOHN CHRYSOSTOM

BUT FRIENDSHIP IS THE BREATHING ROSE,

WITH SWEETS IN EVERY FOLD.

Oliver Wendell Holmes